Colouring in Guernica

Kevin Cadwallender

Red Squirrel Press

First published in the UK in 2007
by Red Squirrel Press
PO BOX 219 MORPETH NE61 9AU
www.redsquirrelpress.com

Guernica images by Charlie Cadwallender

Back cover photo by Deborah Murray

ISBN 978-0-9554027-1-5

©Kevin Cadwallender 2007

All rights reserved.

Kevin Cadwallender has asserted his rights under the Copyright Designs and Patents Act, 1988 to be identified as the author of this work.

Printed in the UK by Athenaeum Press Ltd.
Gateshead, Tyne & Wear

Some of these poems or versions of POEMS have appeared in Artery, Moodswing, Orbis, Other Poetry, Yakker, Morden Poets, Get Rhythm, BBC Radio 4/Soundscape Production, 'Voyages' and on Franks Casket website and Interpoetry Website. Bee Postcards. Rewiring Houdini (Bee Books). The South face of Groucho Marx (with Aidan Halpin, Sand Press). 'Stake Out' was commissioned by Durham County Council Libraries and Museums. 'This Tyne' was commissioned by One North East via New Writing North. 'Removed' was commissioned for Ek Zuban's 'The Wilds' book. Thanks to the editors of those.

Dedicated to the memory of John Cadwallender.
And as always to my children
Matt, Shani and Charlie.

Contents

Colouring in Guernica	1
The Lost Art of Catching Trains	3
At Some Point in Time We Fractured	4
Mc Genesis	5
Paradise Lost	8
Radio Grammar:	
A) The Home Service	9
b) Caroline	10
c) The World Service	11
d) Luxembourg	12
e) The Light Programme	13
An Apoplexy for Poetry	14
This Tyne	18
Instructions for the Obsolete:	
i) The Camera	20
William Blake on the Never Never	21
Haute Couture & the Bias Cut	22
Phil and Don	24
Urbanal	26
The Archaeology of Shopping	29
The Poetry Register	30
Bad Children's Poem	33
The Blood of Hales	35
Stake Out	36
Traditional	38
Foreign Bodies	39
Instructions for the Obsolete:	
ii) Love	40
The Lost Boys	41

Coffee and the corners of the heavens.	42
Everything sounds like Kurt	43
Another Diary Entry	44
The Phrenology of Paint	45
Instructions for the Obsolete:	
iii) Having Children	46
There are loads of planets with a North	48
Removal (i)	51
Removed	52
Murieston Crescent	53
Dances with Vowels	54
Imagine Nation	56
Recoil	58
The Edge of the World	59
Jerusalem Giant	60
The Transit of Venus	61
Instructions for the Obsolete:	
(iv) Sex	62
Clocks	64
Instructions for the Obsolete:	
(v) Death	65

Colouring in Guernica

Take out your books and brains
You are going to experience art
whether you want to or not.
Well it's bit dull but it's only
a photograph of a painting.
And a black and white one at that,
I bet the colours are spectacular like Gaudi
Yes, Gaudi's the one whose buildings
look like melted candles in theTapas bar
on Gray Street, He was Italian or Spanish and
dead I think. Was that a cathedral?
I thought it was a painting!
What's it called? funny name,
The Sagrada Family something or other.
I've got it, well not it,
No, a postcard, from my ex
Unfinished really (not my ex he's finished)
A bit of a building site not like ours
No, not like ours...
Here are the felt tips and
For those of you who aren't allowed felt tips
Because of the spontaneous graffiti project
workshop we had in last week and the incident in
the corridor washable pens and Crayons.
Now then pay attention
we are here to learn something.
Let's imagine what colours Picasso used
In colouring in his famous painting, *Guernica*
Obviously it's about War
And War as you will all know is a bad thing

And none of you must start one,
Use lots of red and orange
Here is the blue in case
you want sky but we have run out of yellow
But that's okay because we don't need sunshine
today. Ignore the lightbulb in the top left corner
of the picture let's pretend it's not switched on.
I will order more yellow soon.
Try not to draw both eyes on the side like Picasso
because it's silly and we don't look like that.

You don't need to know anything about art to
teach it, my boyfriend is a painter... and decorator
Last week we had fun and education
Joining the dot to dots
on Starry starry night by Don McLean
And drawing alien arms
on the Venus Di Milo by Leonardo Di Caprio.

Now children,you see this man here
Impersonating *Edward Munch's* 'The Scream'
He is our visitor today and he will teach you
Everything there is to know about poetry
He doesn't have a real job like me
And his name is Kevin.

The Lost Art of Catching Trains

You learn from hobos
The art of catching trains
Rod McKuen

Terminal,
These feelings,
Limping, crippled pigeons
Pecking at pasty crusts.
Under Victorian
Raised eyebrows.

Written on time and tagged
onto the railway embankment,
Inch"
Size has meaning;
every shudder of graffiti,
a body falling into electricity.

Pushing myself to the platform's edge,
closing my eyes, feeling for raised
warning circles through my soles
as we hurtle in foetal chairs out
of this particular auricle of darkness

over river on rivet and metal.
or swaying like bruised fruit,
ready to drop, waiting for
green lights in our minds
and at our fingers.
Control is given to us;
a relieved sigh as doors part.

an exchange of audiences

a ticket to deride
platform shoes
ho ho ho
By a less than grand Central Station
I sat down and wept for
the lost art of catching trains
and letting them go.

At Some Point in Time We Fractured

at some point in time we fractured,
uncertain of which bones to break
we broke them all.
climbed walls
without fear
of falling.
at some point in time we fractured.
uncertain of which promises to break
we broke them all
and being unable to keep broken promises,
we made new ones.

Not all the king's horses
nor all the king's men
have our vanity.

Mc Genesis

'and he shall bring the bullock unto the door of the tabernacle of the congregation...and shall lay his hand upon the bullock's head, and kill the bullock'

There is no God but McGod
And Ronald is his prophet.

And the lord spake unto Ronald saying
Make thee burgers of undisclosed ingredients
and fat content and distribute them among the
punters and build me a double neon golden arch
to commemorate me on every hillside
and on every industrial estate
So that my people shall know where
to gather in my worship
And let them taste the communion of the
cheeseburger and the coke
And shun the temptations of Pepsi
And Ronald was content with this
Building the double arc of the covenant
As a promise to man that never again would he
be without cholesterol.

And McGod instructed Ronald
for the second time
Saying gather me acolytes of the spotty
and the acned variety that they may spit
upon the burgers of the unrighteous
And dress them in the robes and
raiment of baseball priests
And let them be monosyllabic
at the sacred windows of ordering

And Ronald ensured that his disciples
were dull and lifeless and incapable of
stringing a sentence together and
McGod looked upon the scene
and deemed it regular.

And then McGod spake once more
and for the last time to Ronald
Telling him to adorn his face with the white
greasepaint and generally frighten the children
with the twisting of balloons
and pointless juggling
For Old McDonald is a jealous god
(and hath a beef farm called South America)
And Ronald was wroth and
other things ending in oth
but not broth, obviously
And threatened plagues
of sesame seeds and indeed
Poppy seeds that catcheth
in your teeth or dentureth
And a scourge of cardboard fries
That shall be as dead as the dead sea
in terms of salt and…. deadness.

'for I bring not forth food
for the pleasure of the tongue
nor food that will please the likes of you
but pap that will sustain you
for the pap you shall live through,
and Ronald smiled
and was well in with the Disney franchise

saying 'for the people of the mouse
shall be our brethren'
and we shall deliver the holy burger until
the ancient Celtic religion
of Fishanchip is no more
and the Big Mac shall lie down with the lamb
and maketh the kebab burger and those who
partake of the drive thru communion
shall sit on the right hand of our father McDonald
who farts in Heaven without the aid of soya
Repeat after me......

There is no god but McGod
and he shall make a profit.

Ah man!

Paradise Lost

We were never ones for Paradise
If I gave you an apple you'd only eat it.
And our naked majesty, no doubt
Would be marred by your stretch
Marks and my paunch.

So it's best to stick to what we know
I'm not keen on gardening and Eden
would soon be overgrown.

Let paradise stay lost
Only look to find us,
Falling,
Falling all the way
To Heaven.

Radio Grammar

a) The Home Service

Nothing to do with holding anything together.
The tearing of bed sheets so that we have
a piece of what we deserve.

Nothing to do with love or
the discarded promises
that line the passages
we forced ourselves to navigate
because it was something to do with duty.

Nowhere is it written
that you are great and I am small
or reversing this fraction and
canceling out all things to
be considered and coming
to a conclusion, finally.

Nowhere is a difficult place
to find something,
is the first place to
look if you have nothing.

nothing to do with me if you love me
you said, leaving me zero.
My head dropped.
Oh! I murmured,
What? you asked.
Nothing I replied.

b) Caroline

Caroline, songs lashed to your mast
everything lacks salt these days
and the swash and buckle
are lost in schedules and play lists.

I was a boy when you cross boned
my skull into rebellion,
raising a flag that we
forget to raise enough.

I have it here in my sea chest
anarchy, revolution and liberty
written in biro and felt tip
still legible.

Play one last song for me,
Caroline,
before scurvy
puts paid to us all.

c) The World Service

God that voice
announcing it casually,
just like that as
if it was really were...

This is the world service

as if every one hearing it
would know the innate
superiority of the British,
nay the English by accent alone.
As if a blind man
can tell a Rolex
by touch and sound.
Odd that

This is the world service

felt like a linguistic headmaster
patronizing my colonial dialect,
God that voice!
I would know it anywhere,
like being caught
with your fingers
in the tuck shop till.

Writing poetry,
waiting for the drawer
to slam shut.,

d) Luxembourg

At night under the cliché
of sheets and a torch
listening to the crackle and buzz
of ether leaking between songs.
You whispered into my teenage ear
like a lover, touched me
where I touched myself.

Now, with the North Sea
making hush noises at
every turn and rain
whipping across curved glass,
I hear you again in a car
edging through this digital world.

An unexplained thrill,
A half remembered song,
headlights cutting a storm,
A smile lights up my dial
like valves.

e) The Light Programme

All morning the light had changed instinctively,
Never pausing to contemplate the density of mist
or take in the sunrise growing unseen behind
cloud.

You had folded sheets, talked of linen and your
laughter floated over the room like petals.

On the radio that morning
listeners relayed poetry,
Forgotten poets stirred
in vanquished slumber
Raising their heads into
the living's consciousness.

You had made tea, put my breakfast before me,
Even though sadness
caressed your shoulders
like a shawl.

The day progressed as usual.
The train left.
I drove away.
You were in your head and in mine.
Neither of us would forget.

The light drained out of the sky
as if a plug had been pulled.

An Apoplexy For Poetry

To begin at the beginning...again
Neither Llareggub nor Terry Street,
Dismal in fasting November,
Rain edges its way down uncleaned glass.
a cat has piled the executed at the front door,
weathered windows cover vision with fog
blurred houses become watercolours.

The see saw of passing sirens
in the city of dog the cats claw .
Neither Peru nor Benidorm
the cultural rot does not concern
the girls who trot the well worn trail
from Cooperage to Est est est
and all the shots fired between.

The candyman's trumpet farts
a fanfare for ghosts and grails
long since rotten on hooks.
Neither tenor bull nor jingling geordie.
the concerns of the literati
De situ septic tankus
and sanctorum bollocks.

Primum cantauit Caedmon
out of tune and out of Durham
where Caddell's bonsai'd work grew.
Neither Guttersnipe
nor the booted Prince of Sparty Lea.

made a single dent in
the armour of hegemony.

As clear as Crystal
The Liar boys turn the earth
rake up reality and the fluvial suspects,
Neither Ultima Thule
nor Eric's axe though sharp
cuts through the great
British indifference.

We are lost
purveyors of cack
local poets and tribal chieftains;
at war with 'the establishment'
but mostly with ourselves.
It is a principle we hold most dear
biting the hand that keeps us in beer.

Empire builders
from the Tyne to the Tees,
and the Wear to the Tweed,
Neither King Ida's Watchchain,
Silken Stand nor Mudfog's attrition.
The passwords for success
are naked and ambition.

New words in their order
and the jukebox plays the bear
Rat arsed in the Crown Posada
Where every poet has an M.A.,
The Iron man in Cullercoats

has wed the Angel of the North,
Fundamental changes alter
the substance of the source.

Runic torches splay and arc
across the Tees Valley,
Pissing where Ginsberg pissed
howling dark in rats alley.
Where smokestack flares
old ideals of underdog menace
reclaiming our tradition
The bards of Vane terrace?

The room was blue
with vagary and about to implode
words kicking at the heels
of Horace's epodes,
dunshing like easter eggs
at Christ knows who's tomb.
We are the weather forecasters
Of poetic doom.

And the Vandals only reached the door
And chalked their names in lightly
Crushed by the great indifference
Court Jesters of the Muse Almighty.
The sheep are spelling out the names
Of those tipped for posterity.
The dye runs down their fleeces
And robs us of all clarity.

The great the good,

The ear of wood,
The brave , the bold,
The ones whose souls
Were all but sold
For Acne gold.
Left in the cold
as foretold.

To end at the end and seek to stand
Our boots in this acknowledged land
We are rutting in the trough of shit
For a mouthful of the holy tit.
The work-shopped out
The nothing to say
All queue to fight
For equal pay.

Bunting's ghost at Swan Hunter's gate
Beleaguered by the Welfare State
Where poets sign the dotted line
For a chance to sell their pearls to swine.

Griffith's line in Seaham fell
Summit bizen-clivor scunnered Hell
a rammel lobbed into the coal kibble
now all this yowlin turns to scribble

An apoplexy for poesy
A fait accompli for no one knows
And beyond it, the deep blue air, that shows
Nothing but the raucous cackle of crows.

This Tyne

the gramophone in the Crown Posada
scratches out George Formby
whose wife never let kiss his leading ladies,
but I would kiss you.
We drift along the quayside like untethered boats
touching, barging, jostling ,
Your faith is unsinkable.
We are slow mourners
heads low up Dog Leap Stairs
pausing to forget to kiss
under the viaducts at Castle Keep
and deep into the day and into our pockets
we drink in one corner
or another of The Bridge Hotel.
This Tyne that flows like ale over dreamers.

I am waiting for
unrequited love at Central Station
It is a train that never stops arriving.
Her text is enigmatic she is tardy
a word I found in 'O' level Lear
but almost appropriate here
in the tiled splendour of the Centurion.
she drives my bonnie dreams away
I keep my feet as still as bed linen
My heart is happy through the night.

Victoria Regina sits looking
up the skirts on the Bigg Market
from her throne outside of St.Nicks,

no Alberts in sight
but plenty of Tom, Dicks and Debbies.
From bar to bar to bar,
searching for a taste of what we are,
and love is kebab cheap
or brief in the darkness
of a hire purchased car.
and the fog on the Tyne is
a timeshare investment.

The girl in the Windows arcade is singing Verdi.
the poets huddle in the Tower behind the Gate
Newcastle is no longer just a city of starlings.
Morrissey mentioned Skipsey at the City Hall
lost on his disciples, apostles of the shopping
mall.

I am drinking cooking lager in the Crown Posada
Listening to George Formby,
whose leading ladies were never kissed
Evangelists and minstrels merge at Monument,
The clear white light looks blue.
Grainger Town is about to cast off
its concrete overcoat and dance.
Naked as the Baltic, the Sage's mirrored snail.

This Tyne, from now
until forever running
Between you and me.

Instructions for the Obsolete

i) The Camera

Externalise the component part.
(take it out of the box!)

Instigate the electric to the power of 4
(put batteries in it)

Secure the start up position by indexing the power switch
(turn it on)

Manually reset for optimum usage,
(if it doesn't work bang it on a table)

With dexterity of digit utilise your index representative to captivate the positive switch.
(use your finger to press the fucking button)

Imaging is formally over
(you have taken a picture)

Manufacturer's guidance at base of product.
(address to send it back to).

William Blake on the Never Never

Insomnia
all those red bills
pecking at his sleep,
wondering
if William Blake
had cause to worry,
knowing the text book answer
to that,
If his wife
coming down to breakfast
unpeeled the world,
his skin with a single
well placed knife.

'You might write a best selling novel'
or
'Bill, Bill the cupboard is bare'
His ghosts in their paint and splendour
sniggering behind empty palates,
'Get a job, make more money'

I have seen him
in that Victorian waistcoat
fumbling with a pawnable watch;
I move through Sainsburys
my credit card cuts through hunger
like a genius.

'There's an advert here for a painter and
decorator'

Haute Couture & The Bias Cut

(It is only shallow people who
do not judge by appearances: Oscar Wilde)

Haute couture clumps on Ferragamo wedges
On the busy underground puking out of Baker
Street.........

Commuters in Howell tweeds
and Bowerman sports
Squeezed into caviar clothes
and Macdonald mohair burgers.

On the Portobello Road
Stella McCartney dipping for bargains
The icons are branded by cattle barons
in New York and London

And in the rue Cambon where Coco ripped
off her dress sleeves to grasp the iron
The milkman delivers milk
in Calvin Klein boxer shorts.
Fashion; for a definition
the collision of nothing
and everything,

George has his feet under the check-out.
Hard to stomach but easy to swallow,

Laura Ashley's rural idyll.
Perfume that fades into sweat

Pierre Cardin dresses Captain Kirk.
A train crashes into a row of mannequins

A massacre of Twiggys .
Under the sound of Bow bells

Dumb Armani wearing pimps
Bray into mobiles .

Fiorucci size women
Wearing Harry size jewels,

Beauty and the savage breast.
Applique as subtle as poetry.

London thinks with its face
As quaint as Quant
And as laughable as Sassoon.

Handbags at twenty paces
And the sound of chiffon teased
Over Versace's dead face.

Phil and Don
(*for Chris Storey*)

Brothers under our skinful,
cheerfully downing schnapps and cheap lager.

hurtling headlong into our gig
on porcelain french horns.

Us twin Dylan Thomasi,
arrogant Gemini,

Pissed as Romulus and Remus
wolfing magic mushrooms.

Too far starry
in dandelion days.

Me and you and George,
busking Beatles songs

outside of the 'Gamecock'
after I'd been thrown

out of the Conservative club
for kissing a woman

and pouring lager
over a union jack.

and you a failed lightweight
pinned by that fat committee man

making your own canned laughter
as he tried to punch your head off.

Those days are gone.
The Wind has dispersed our seed at fall

Our heads bobbing above the alcohol
that has flowed over our bridgework.

Two reprobates
with kids, divorce and debt.

but once we were
the Everly Brothers

of vomit.

URBANAL

We have already bought the t shirts
they say
'God Wears Burberry'
They will appeal to all demographics,
youth culture , women's institutes,
they will sell like hot cakes.
we will sell hot cakes too,
(they will sell like t-shirts.)

On the allotment someone
has pulled the head off a pigeon
it blinks once as its body attempts flight.
I don't like this world much.
I throw up on Gary's new combats,
he scrapes it off with a Bowie knife.
Named after the famous Byker Wall
frontiersman Bob Knife.

I once pissed on a homeless gadgey
when I was an anarchist, whispers Kieron
But I was younger then and full of principles.
Time is elastic and stretches to fit me in
like a cervix, states Gregg
who says he is a film maker,
although he has never actually made a film
 although he has now made a poem
(although this is open to dispute)
although is an overused word and works badly
under repetition
although...........

Billy is an Ulsterman
his accent does not give him away
who wants to know why we would assume he was
a protestant.

What part of Ireland do you come from?

The North!

Yes, but which part of the North?

Erm ....Limerick

Limerick's in the South....I think

Yes well, it's a long way from Tipperary

Actually, it's just not

we reckon he's half Irish.
Half Irish and half wank.

Michael comes in and reminds me of a joke poem
that hardly anybody ever gets. it depends on a
knowledge of T.S.Eliot, Adam Faith and Inspector
Jack Regan;
We call it Sweeney among the Budgerigars
'Get your strides on Budgie, you're nicked!'
we laugh like pretentious drains.
I am explaining the joke to
a seventeen year old Darlington supporter
He looks at me with a blank expression

I look at him with an empty glass
neither of us takes the hint.

Amelia is a woman of many faces
I don't like any of them.
She looks like a young Glenda Jackson
Her mother looks like an old Glenda Jackson..
Amelia you are the ghost of alienation,
false as alarms you wear
the hexagram of the 7/11
plucking Day-Glo strings and feathers,
and I, am Icarus with Daedalus envy.

The morning cracks under interrogation
the loaf I bought this morning smells of vinegar,
angels shoplift featherlite
condoms from superdrug
wings hidden under coats borrowed from the
cursed and charmed and others of us who are
truly alarmed

Captain Black is leaving
for the last metro
I drink up and follow.
A drunk teenager mistakes me
for Troy Tempest
as I make for the exit.

I didn't think her generation would remember.

These are the days of indolence and expedience.

The Archaeology of Shopping

Always one wheel
that cannot be explained,

part of the history deal,
nothing censored, nothing gained.

We are searching,
our eyes are mattocks,

randy with hacking
and let us prussock

this half-baked hill of beans.
These aisles, not churches,

pews of produce and price-cuts,
this cage on castors lurches

passed the check out operator's pulpit.
No holy brimstone, hallelujah

     only stamps
to get you into heaven's Xmas club.

Buying no divine light
but cheap lamps

to lighten the collection
of cheque book stubs.

The Poetry Register

Acrostic
Alliteration..alliteration..alliteration ...Thank you.
pay attention
Ambiguity..ambiguity Look are you here or not?.
　　　　　　　Make up your mind..here..fine.
Assonance
Bard
Bathos
Blake ... Blake. I've warned you before about screen printing in registration..what is it anyway? *'The ghost of a flea'*. Detention.
Clerihew　　　....
Cliché . Cliché you are an accident waiting to happen!
Correlative
Cooper-Clarke ..sunglasses off in school ,boy.
Dactyl ...
Diphthong...late again..
Didactic　...
Doggerel – Silence!
Things just go from bad to verse
with you don't they boy?
Epithalamion .. Is he here?
Absent. Gone to Parents wedding.
Fuck....sorry. He's been excluded.
Grant ..Welcome to the new boy.
(His Father built the west wing)
Gibberish the Elder
Gibberish the Younger
Haiku

Hegley I don't care if it's not a banjo put it down
Hughes
Hyperbole ' Fine ' in the future please replace
'here until the seas run dry' with a
        functional yes.
Iambic
Jabberwocky Come to my arms, I mean office later.
Kubla khan ; put that away finish it later.
Limerick
Lottery
Lyric
The Muse triplets
Metaphor
Nonsense
Onomatopoeia – what do you mean 'Booing.'
a simple Yes will suffice.
Oxymoron
Ozymandias
Pentameter
Parody and Plagiarism – you two report to the Head after registration. We are not as stupid as we look.
Plath
Polemic . when I want your opinion I'll give you it.
Rap..rap There's nothing big or clever about swearing .
Renga
Rhyme – Nice to see you back.
I hope you're better this time.
Sestet

Sestina
Simile. *Simile!* What are you like boy? .
Slam
Sonnet
Tanka
Tradition
Trochee
Typo
Under Milk Wood Junior
Villanelle
Workshop and
Xanadu Ah yes…. Xanadu
Our poetry-geography crossover.
Yeats
Zephaniah.

Dismiss!

Bad Children's Poem

This is my bad children's poem
It goes (raspberry noise) in all of the right places!
It says teachers stink and goes BANG! Twice.
This is my children's poem
It doesn't like to go to school
It likes to eat Pizzas
And Happy Meals,
It thinks dinner ladies
Smell of cabbage,
Everyone shout 'Poo!'
It has competitions in the boys toilets
To see who can pee the highest
It throws waterbombs at lollipop ladies
It says 'ourfatherwhichfartsinheaven'
during assembly
It pulls pigtails and ponytails
And BANG! (Told you it went Bang Twice!)
And then it swears and
Ooh miss did you hear that?
It called me a bumbag, miss
Everyone shout , 'Poo!'
And it isn't really about anything
And it doesn't listen when it is spoken to
And it spits like a granddad
And it eats snots or wipes them on someone
else's jumper,
And it likes to stay up late
And watch Pop idol
Or play on its Play Station 2
Grand Theft Auto 27

And it falls asleep in maths lessons
And eats too much chocolate
At playtime miss and
is sick as a parrot
And likes Dr.Pepper
And Harry Potter
And cheers at hometime miss
And tells lies
And poohs its pants
Phor!
Everyone say pooh!
BANG ! that's more than twice
what a liar!
That was three times.
And it finishes just when
You want it to keep going.

- *Italics : lines nicked from the greatest children's poem ever which isn't really for children but should be 'Please Miss' by Mike Dillon.*

The Blood of Hales

'the bloud of Hales did so long blynd the Kynge': Latimer

These are the days of miracles and wonder
or at least I am led to believe that a miracle
is the province of the unspectacular,
A man on a cross replaced by a man in a box,
symbols of the fall from grace,

There are four corners on a cross
and four corners on a box
states a believer.

I happily point out that
a box has eight corners
and that a square is not a box

he looks at me like a collie
trying to understand philosophy
whilst gazing at a lamb chop.

I slip him from his leash
I have set him free to run under cars
It is called free will.
He could have chosen a Rolls Royce
but a Ford Fiesta will do the job just as well.

Don't look at me like that
God created me too you'd say
Although he hasn't
sewn his nametag
into my shirt.

Stake Out
(for Pam Kindred)

Not knowing where to begin
is a great place to start
Take your tongue out of my cheek
and the stake out of my art.

I'll be crafty in my sullen room
and sharpen up my stick
With my psalms at the ready
for the dead and the not, so, very, quick.

I'll be resident and not at home,
available and keen
The life and soul of the library,
heard and obscene,

I'll be running though your headlines
and rhyming on TV
Hot off the local radio
the ventriloquist doll and me!

'Poets' you'll say don't matter
and poetry's just for school
Take your stake out of my art
while I trash a few old rules,

Poetry dancing in the clubs
with the rightful owners of the voices
Iambic in the back of taxis and rhythmic
in the front of Rolls Royces.

Bring me your sick your lame,
bring me your huddled masses,
I'll bludgeon them with the miracle
of creative writing classes.

A tongue in your cheek and a word in your ear
A tongue in your cheek and a word in your ear

I'll be crafty in my sullen room
and sharpen up my stick
With my psalms at the ready
for the dead and the not so very quick.

Not knowing where to finish
is a great place to end
Take this stake out of my art
and unzip another trend

Shot right off the bookshelves squirming on TV
Hot off the wireless the spoon bender and me

I'll be quick I'll be quaint
I'll get the scansion right
I won't make the line too long and stick in
irrelevant things about politics like other poets
                                        might.

A tongue in your cheek and a word in your ear
A tongue in your cheek and a word in your ear.

Tongue. Cheek. Word. Ear.

Stake. Art. Out. Over.

Stake. Art. Out. Over.

Stake, Out…

over and out.

Traditional

The traditions of the North
Are coal and ships and labour,
With annoying bagpipe music
To accompany this behaviour.

Foreign Bodies

You say,
I should send you to Leicester for that!
I say,
You mean Coventry.
you say,
I've never been to Coventry.
I say,
Maybe we should go together.

After that
we may as well have.

Golden is silenced
she whispers

in an accent as unfamiliar as
Leicester's less famous cathedral.

My wife doesn't understand me.
I tell you in desperation,
You say,
Where is she from?
why did you marry someone
who doesn't speak English?
I say,
That's not what I meant
fumbling for an alibi that
transcends language.

Instructions for the Obsolete

ii) Love

Initiate primary selection of
correct gender disciple
(Choose a woman)
Reschedule compatibility Quotient
(or a man)
Assume the notion of perfect symmetry of facial
characteristics
(choose someone beautiful)
Optic assimilation may not
concur with current opinion
(beauty is in the eye of the beholder)
Declaim intentionally as objectified
Witnesses the process
(talk to her)
Reject borrowed attire
and extinguish negative linguistics
(Be yourself and don't lie)
Convey emotive speech content
(Tell her how you feel)
Synchronise your wonder
(love her)
Until expiration date.
(until you die).

The Lost Boys
(for Aidan Halpin)

We must learn to hold it together
accept our inability to be charming,
accept the girth of our wit is proportionate
to half the girth of our waistlines,
accept this riposte from the latest
barmaid as par,
accept that calling her a barmaid may
have queered the pitch
accept that our terminology is due for revision,
accept that the 'kids on the street'
are our children or worse our children's children.
Learn that growing old disgracefully
is a synonym for growing old ridiculously,
Learn to shrug at ageism
Learn to adopt the mannerisms of those
we mocked when we were the 'enfant terrible'
and learn that we were as inane and banal
as the current 'enfant terrible'.
We will grow to be lost if we do not,
and Peter Pan although the world's role model
is as lost as us and twice as scared.
We will grow wise and wear slippers with zips,
We will grow water bottles in our beds
We will grow ear and nasal hair
We will grow up into our parents
and these young bastards with no respect
have got it coming to them and
serve them right.
We will grow the nerve to move to

the first person;
I will grow and accept and learn
although I have decided never to stoop
so low as to validate my love for the lost
boys that have come and gone.

Coffee and the corners of the heavens.
(for Louise Dal)

You must be careful what you say,
The strangest of seeds will take root,

You must be careful what you touch,
Some pieces of her are fragile.

I watch the way she moves, assured
Of her place under this heaven.

The way she stirs coffee, holds the spoon
Between indelicate fingers.

Surprising, considering her
Songs both strange and soul unfulfilled,

Yet rising like love in the heart
And moving me to her defence,

That all these creatures at her light
Do not notice these corners of night.

Everything sounds like Kurt

Not that it matters but I have heard of 'Nirvana'
When my son says things like, 'Jimi Hendrix was
quite good', I try not to shudder.
Not that I care much about three chord anthems
that share a similarity to the three chord anthems
I hail as better and view through
my window of rosé tinted clarity.

My Father once said to me ,
'What is this rubbish?'
To 'Mott the Hoople' or some such band.
So I don't say it, though I often think it
when music becomes banal or bland.

I'm the right age and cynical enough
To line up with the Jazz buffs
Though Blues men think it odd
My lack of faith that 'Blind Willie' is God,

And at the local folk club
where the ghost of Ewan MacColl sneers
I dutifully put my finger in my ear
and in both ears when I finish my beer.

'Everything sounds like Kurt'
Snorted with teenage disgust
at some sound-alike trend
'Weill?' I offer with a hint of redemption,

'Exactly' he says and 'crap' as well.

Another Diary Entry
(for and after Edwin Brock)

I was suspicious of Brock's violins
And could not tell if Magnolia was white

Or if the tough dogs ripping at the
Woodwork in Mowbray Gardens

Were dangerous.
Ultimately, or not as the seasons

Turned us inside out, the buggies
And pushchairs we manoeuvred

Through the chess men clutching
Brown paper bibles were carrying

Other Edens in their clever
Collapsible hearts.

Ours had been padlocked up
For the winter and the old men

With woods clacking like
Their teeth were wearing black

At the church yard and
Emptying mothballs and

Blossom petals
Out of wide lapelled suits

With once dashing bags
Flagging like ensigns

At stork thin legs.

The Phrenology of Paint

I have been trailing light fingers
over the surface of oils;

Following the landscape of uneven ridges.
Absent of colour, these strokes

need to be art through other devices.
I am splaying my palms over textures

trying to detect the ripple of matter.
The brain that made this,

The creator identified in the created,
The smudged index of God

encoded in bone.
Here are my epiphanies;

Absence of vision is not darkness.
Absence of god is not emptiness.

I open my eyes
And take for granted.

Instructions for the Obsolete

iii) Having Children

Initiate primary selection of
correct gender disciple
(Choose a woman)
Reschedule compatibility Quotient
(or a man)

Selection of Male in this instance may eradicate
objective if you are also Male.
See Adoption.
See handbook ii) Love and
Handbook   iv) Sex

Enjoy the prequel of ecstatic ritual
(it will be fun making them)

Repetition of ecstatic ritual
(Wa hey! You're screwed!)

Process and clearance will be three quarters of
the annual retinue.
(It takes nine months to have a baby)

Warning:
Post Natal Coitus Interruptus
may terminate further ecstatic ritual
(you are screwed.)

Initial response may contra indicate product
presence.
(you'll wish you never bothered)

Insomnia may be rendered consistently
(you won't sleep)

Bi annually
(for at least two years)

Constantly regulate nocturnal emissions
(listen for your baby crying)

Emit low tech dental expression
(gnash your teeth)

Defoliate hirsutely
(pull your hair out)

Resonate grief
(cry)

Bi annually
(for about two years)

Regrets will be decommissioned
by temporal dispersion
(You won't regret any of it, given time)

See Clause 3 'Teenagers'
(which may invalidate
all warranties and guarantees.)

There are loads of planets with a North

It doesn't make me a hero ,
or an alien doctor from the BBC
It's just a part of what I am
and a part of who I claim to be,
Time and relative distance
in space from the naughty north
to the sexy south and all this
is relative to where you are
of course.

There are loads of planets with a north

And I live in the south to the Scots
who espouse that I'm just English
and there is no difference and borderline's
are arbitrary and part of this condition
In Lapland they would laugh in the face of a
Glaswegian (stupidly)
if they said they were northern
and geography is the rules
they teach you in school,
so assume the position.

There are loads of planets with a North

Just because you say something
doesn't make it so,
Turning the world upside
down exchanges one pole
for another pole,

From compass pointless arguments
about history and tradition
the London scene appoints its leaders
and they begin an expedition.
To teach us what we know inherently to be true
that labels like North and South
have got everything to do
with the landscape of redundant issues,
with the way you say your vowels
and they layer on the patronage
with linguistic whoops and howls.
There are lots of planets with a north
and just as many with a south
Some times it seems it's just a case of who
or maybe whom has the biggest mouth,
I would shout it from the rooftops
but I may be misunderstood
I could buy a whippet and a flat cap
they say it's in my blood
I have been flattening my vowels
like Chaucer did before me
If I talk in my own dialect
why do some people ignore me?

I am for richness, diversity
of speech and thought
Ignorance is only knowing your place,
poverty is a label that can't be bought
I am a product of years
of nurturing this industrial chip
on a shoulder meant for digging coal
and welding bits on ships

So what's the point in industry
when nothing is worth making
It's more than hard to tell a Charv
the can of worms he's waking
and that's a mixed metaphor
if I ever I saw one
I am standing at a crossroads
with my Novocastrian hard on
and Dr.Whoever and whatever
you say goes
but you couldn't catch a cold
with that elitist pose.

It doesn't make me a working class hero
to sigh as David Tennant
suppresses those rich Scots vowels
or him a traitor for his anglicised speeches.
I won't fight him on the beaches
Or castigate linguistic teachers
Or take the piss out of North East creatures
For covering the deck chair
of the Queen's English
With an indecipherable dialect towel.
There are lots of Planets with a North
To misquote the Doctor as this poem aborts.
You can take the man out of the language
But not the language out of the man.

What are we afraid of?
What are parochialists after,
For Charver read chav,
for laffter read laughter.

I digress as words run their course
Dicks for Dictionaries,
Encyclopaedophiles,
Pedants and much worse,
fuck it
There are loads of Planets with a North.
Why aye!

Removal (i)

To empty
From home to home
All the emotional
Furniture and its fixtures.
Package the love,
Parcel memory.

You will find me
At a new address
Should you call.

I know you will not.

Removed

When writing a poem about moving house,
One should not use bric a brac in anyway
And discard the use of 'discard' and try if you
Are at all able not to anthropomorphise your
house.
Don't look back, it will look at you with sad
square eyes
Even the removal men are
having trouble lifting the sentiment
That is gathering in your head.

Having moved once, don't fall into the
Trap of writing about it a second time
The same old empty boxes and yes maybe
Even tea chests
(if you are moving in the Victorian era)
Will appear and you will be forced
to review your possessions
As if they are metaphorical,
They are not and stop thinking of similes for
Unseen clocks ticking in boxes!
Don't you dare use words like 'Flotsam'
And absolutely no to 'Jetsam'.
Lock all doors, watch the walls sighing.

Don't even bother reaching for a pen,
When words like 'nostalgia and memorabilia'
Are near. Get a ladder,
clear the bird's nest out of the guttering.
Avoid titles like 'Home from Home'

Anything but that or 'Once Removed'
The slow decline into pun,
(heading off into the punset)
Thank God it is over
And brace yourself
For the next time.

Tell all your friends how stressful
It has all been, milk their sympathy,
Turn up your collar as you walk past
The man with a dog in the shop doorway,
The Big Issue seller that makes you deaf.
The money in your pocket safe as houses.

Murieston Crescent

The iron of passion
Railings surrounding
My heart as ever, visible
And your dark, troubled waters
Under the cloak of love
We huddled between what
I remember as rain
Although my memory is flawed.
And later in grave circumstance
I trembled at your kiss
That impaled me as
Easily as a butterfly on a pin.

Dances with Vowels

If I had known that *Vowels*
Was an anagram of *Wolves*
Or indeed that *Wolves* was an anagram of *Vowels*
I would have written this a long time ago.

I was raised by a pack of vowels.
Five unrelated aunties
Who gathered around my crib
Reciting the incantation

Aaah
Eeee
Aye
Oh
You.

When I said crib there I wanted to say manger
That might mean I have a God Complex
An inner sublimated Christ rising to the surface
However I am an atheist
Which means I don't know if God exists
Not that I don't care if God exists,
I don't know what Jung would have said about that
Maybe he wouldn't care by now.
Jimmy Young would have said TTFN
An acronym devoid of vowels.

I love You

Has an awful lot of vowels
Except in Text messages
Where it simply says I LY.

If little red Riding Hood's Grandmother
Had been eaten by a vowel I suspect
It would be an 'e.'
I ate an 'e' once but that's a different poem.

I found a bag of consonants in my computer
Just rattling around, I tried to use them
Fffffffff Fffff Kkk
Swearing is rubbish without vowels.
I was raised by vowels

I speak the language
And flatten them like a carpenter making a cross.
My aunts are all dead now nailed into coffins
Howling like Werevowels.

Imagine Nation

Imagine you are going out with a woman
Who you have known for a great part of your life
Imagine you marry that woman and have children.
Imagine yourself being happy.
Imagine happiness becoming an illusion.
Imagine that this woman decides to leave you.
Imagine a house collapsing.
Now Imagine your friends being unsupportive
And backing off like a defensive wall at a free kick.

Imagine this is not about me Imagine this is about you.

Imagine that you cope with that.
Imagine that you carry on living
Despite the urge to not.
Now Imagine that you fall in love
And imagine that she is in love with you
Imagine that you create a child out of love.
Now imagine one of you killing that child.
Imagine what you would do.
Imagine what you would say.
Imagine your friends at the second dead ball
Situation of the match,
Protecting their vitals.

Imagine you just about survive
Imagine your therapist wincing

As you recount your life
over the past three years.
Imagine life going on as it does regardless.

Imagine this is not about me
Imagine this is about you.

Now Imagine this man who has
managed to stay on the pitch
And even met someone new ,
Imagine they have met this someone new before.
Imagine that it is the same someone as before
Imagine things are not perfect
Imagine you are not good enough
Imagine anything you like
Realise you are just imagining.
Imagine that love is simpler than life
Imagine living life with joy and optimism.
Imagine you can make this happen.

And if you can't
Imagine there's no Kevin
It isn't hard to do.

Recoil

I could write a love song, *pull*
With an emotional baby
The trigger, somewhere between the
Bit where I leave and the vow
Where I promise to be true forever *pull*
And I will buy you roses
Over the internet at extreme
Prices because 'ilurveu'
And you would kill me if I didn't.
And I will scribe on the bible
Of romantic love a sonnet
That will break your heart
And leave you at the altar
Pull the trigger

I could write a love song
Poignant, tender, hungry
For your touch. *Pull the trigger*
Time flies
And it means nothing
Are you still mine? *The trigger!*
And I will dedicate it to you
And listen as incessant media play,
Drains the love out of it
Like *pull the trigger*
'*I need your love*
Godspeed your love'
I could write a love song
Sentimentally yours

Pull the trigger
Put your fingers to my lips
And keep me still
Pull the trigger
Put your lips to my fingers
And keep me
Shoot.

The Edge of the World

The edge of the world
And all its strange appointments,
We lock together without words.
The edge of the world
And all its brief conjunctions,
Limited in the framework of years,
We hold hands for five minutes
In one lifetime and never touch again.
I want to tell you that
Things can be different,
That the world is no longer cruel,
Come, we shall tell no more lies
And explore one another
Without fear of the edge of the world.

Jerusalem Giant

Jerusalem Giant,
How many tremble in your jaw?
Trample the world to salt
Before innocent eyes.
This morning we knew
In your templed hour
Is blood and gore
The children who
Sat at your gates
Are old men.
Jerusalem Giant,
How many quiver in your teeth?
Metal with hatred,
Obscene corpses
Litter victory
With rubble.

The Transit of Venus

Love escapes me, the great pacific
ocean lies once again,
From Tahiti Fort with degrees
of longitude we chase moonbeams.
The Captain never sleeps
walking the deck like the ghost of romance
he calculates the heat of the sun and
the coldness of lunatics

What is the distance between love and loss?
What is the gulf that separates
should I call it a chasm?

Venus as the Romans called you
dallying with the earth , your wedding trail drags
in flat, windless climes, your maidens offer
us your rites,
we perform them steadfastly
It is our duty.
Chastity is of little value
Trading in the unspeakable

Obarea, queen of the islands
goddess incarnate, bringer of plantains
hogs and delicious dog.

Love escapes me, the great family of man
that likes to rut in shallow runs
We of greater purpose?
are not eroded by such temptations.

The captain never sleeps, he walks the deck
planets form a diadem at his brow.
What is the distance between love and loss,
loss and the transit of love?

Instructions for the Obsolete

(iv) Sex

*Recommendations for the use of this product are
listed in handbook (ii) Love.*

*Caution: Sex is no guarantee of love or vice
versa.*

Initiate primary selection of
correct gender disciple
(Choose a woman)

Reschedule compatibility Quotient
(or a man)

Initiate appropriate gender disciple response
(hope they choose you)

Assume the notion of perfect symmetry of facial
characteristics
(choose someone beautiful)

Engage serendipity mode
(if you are lucky)

Target acquisition has no bearing on quality
Or efficiency or potential to recycle.
(beautiful people might not shag best
And they won't do it to goits
Like you more than once unless drunk or
deranged)

CAUTION
Correct usage of viable equipment may
inititialize productivity.
See Handbook (iii) Having Children.

Commence repetition of the selected desire
(Shag!)

Latex affected area of gender for precautionary
initiation effects
(Oops.. wear a condom)

Assure climactic change in gender disciple
(I think you know what I mean)

A multiplicity of variants
(lots)

Afterglow may be experienced differently by
participants.
(Men, Lie there at least five minutes before you
rush off and wash your bits).

Clocks

Those minutes with you
Were measured
By the clock

Clocks don't give a fuck
And the time we spent
In making love
Or waking with
Children
Was captured
In segments of
Luminous green
On black
Clocks have no propriety
I lay listening
To our love ticking
And dreamt
A genocide
Of clocks

………And time
Ran,
as it always does

Out.

Instructions for the Obsolete

(v) Death

Warily instigate the life interface cut off switch according to product specifications.

(Just die)

Once interface mode has been de initiated the unit will cease to operate.

(You're dead)

Cessation of module should now be remarked.

(You're still dead)

Product warranty in force for in built irreversible obsolescence.

(You're gonna stay dead, guaranteed)

Belief in God will not invalidate this guarantee
(Belief in god will not validate this guarantee)